Data Literacy
Practitioner's Guide

Colophon

Title:	Data Literacy Practitioner's Guide
Subtitle:	EDF Certification Handout
Authors:	Michel Dekker
Publisher:	Van Haren Publishing, 's-Hertogenbosch
ISBN Hard Copy:	978 94 018 1131 6
Edition:	First edition, first print, March 2024
Design:	Van Haren Publishing, 's-Hertogenbosch
Copyright:	© Van Haren Publishing 2024

For further information about Van Haren Publishing please e-mail us at: info@vanharen.net or visit our website: www.vanharen.net

No part of this publication may be reproduced in any form by print, photo print, microfilm or any other means without written permission by the publisher. Although this publication has been composed with much care, neither author, nor editor, nor publisher can accept any liability for damage caused by possible errors and/or incompleteness in this publication.

Other publications by Van Haren Publishing

Van Haren Publishing (VHP) specializes in titles on Best Practices, methods and standards within four domains:
- IT and IT Management
- Architecture (Enterprise and IT)
- Business Management and
- Project Management

Van Haren Publishing is also publishing on behalf of leading organizations and companies: ASLBiSL Foundation, BRMI, CA, Centre Henri Tudor, Gaming Works, IACCM, IAOP, IFDC, Innovation Value Institute, IPMA-NL, ITSqc, NAF, KNVI, PMI-NL, PON, The Open Group, The SOX Institute.

Topics are (per domain):

IT and IT Management
ABC of ICT
ASL®
CATS CM®
CMMI®
COBIT®
e-CF
ISO/IEC 20000
ISO/IEC 27001/27002
ISPL
IT4IT®
IT-CMF™
IT Service CMM
ITIL®
MOF
MSF
SABSA
SAF
SIAM™
TRIM
VeriSM™

Enterprise Architecture
ArchiMate®
GEA®
Novius Architectuur Methode
TOGAF®

Business Management
BABOK ® Guide
BiSL® and BiSL® Next
BRMBOK™
BTF
EFQM
eSCM
IACCM
ISA-95
ISO 9000/9001
OPBOK
SixSigma
SOX
SqEME®

Project Management
A4-Projectmanagement
DSDM/Atern
ICB / NCB
ISO 21500
MINCE®
M_o_R®
MSP®
P3O®
PMBOK ® Guide
Praxis®
PRINCE2®

For the latest information on VHP publications, visit our website: www.vanharen.net.

1 Course overview

As kids, we learned our native language: reading, writing, and speaking. You learn a language by starting with grammar, trying it out, making mistakes and improving it.
We are flooded with facts and figures daily, but how well do we understand the meaning behind all those numbers? How can we turn this data into value in our day-to-day work and for the organization we work for? The ability to derive meaningful information from data is called Data Literacy. Making sense of data is no longer just a skill for data scientists and technology experts but an essential skill for all of us.

Data Literacy is the ability to read, work with, analyze and argue with data.

This course is the first step to make you aware of Data Literacy (as an essential skill) and how it impacts your work. You'll learn the fundamentals and how they relate to working in a data-informed organization. This will be enough for some people to raise the required questions when confronted with data. For others, this is the first step in becoming a fluent data speaker.

The training consists of four modules, each with its own weight towards the certification exam:

	Weight	Topic
Introduction		Introduction to Data Literacy
Read data	25%	The ability to read and interpret data correctly. Which questions we need to ask to avoid fooling ourselves.
Work with data	25%	What happens to data during its journey from the source to final consumption? How does this impact the understanding and possibilities of this data?
Analyze data	25%	Data needs to be analyzed, not only read. In this section we'll have a closer look at how we analyze data.
Argue with data	25%	Once we have found interesting insights in the data, we need to share this with our audience. In this part we'll look at what we need to do so our audience understands the data in the best possible way.

1	COURSE OVERVIEW	4
2	INTRODUCTION	8
3	**READ DATA**	**10**
3.1	**What is data?**	**10**
3.1.1	Data scales	11
3.1.2	Why do we use data?	13
3.2	**Summarize data**	**14**
3.2.1	Central tendency	15
3.2.2	How to summarize data	17
3.3	**Consume data**	**18**
3.3.1	CHRTTS	19
3.3.2	Categorical charts	22
3.3.3	Hierarchical charts	23
3.3.4	Relational charts	24
3.3.5	Temporal charts	25
3.3.6	Tabular cCharts	26
3.3.7	Spatial charts	27
3.4	**Check your data**	**28**
4	**WORK WITH DATA**	**32**
4.1	**Creating data**	**32**
4.1.1	Automated data	32
4.1.2	Manual data	32
4.2	**Data quality**	**33**
4.2.1	Data quality dimensions	33
4.2.2	Avoid confusing data	35
4.3	**Acquiring & cleaning data**	**36**
4.3.1	Tidy data	37
4.3.2	Combine data	38
4.4	**Managing data**	**39**
4.4.1	KPI mantras	40
5	**ANALYZE DATA**	**43**
5.1	**Expectations**	**43**
5.2	**Thinking shortcuts**	**43**

5.2.1	Confirmation bias	45
5.2.2	Survivorship bias	45
5.2.3	Curse of knowledge	45
5.2.4	Correlation vs causation	46
5.3	**Types of analysis**	**47**
5.3.1	Descriptive analysis	47
5.3.2	Diagnostic analysis	48
5.3.3	Inferential analysis	48
5.3.4	Predictive analysis	49
5.3.5	Prescriptive analysis	51
5.4	**Analytical skills**	**51**
5.4.1	Variations within categories	52
5.4.2	Relations among categories	53
5.4.3	Variations within measures	53
5.4.4	Relations among measures	54
5.4.5	Look for patterns	55
6	**ARGUE WITH DATA**	**58**
6.1	**Explore to explain**	**58**
6.1.1	The data cut	59
6.1.2	The data cameo	59
6.1.3	The data decoration	60
6.2	**Effective data visualization**	**61**
6.3	**Storytelling with data**	**62**
6.3.1	The Storytelling Arc	62
6.3.2	Visual storytelling principles	64
7	**FURTHER READING**	**72**

2 Introduction

When asked, most of us recognize data in the workplace as an asset. This was clearly demonstrated in "The Human Impact of Data Literacy" study in 2020 where 87% of employees recognized data as an asset.

But if we ask employees whether they trust their decisions more when based on data, only 37% says "yes". And when asked about confidence in their own data literacy skills, only 21% confirmed this was the case.

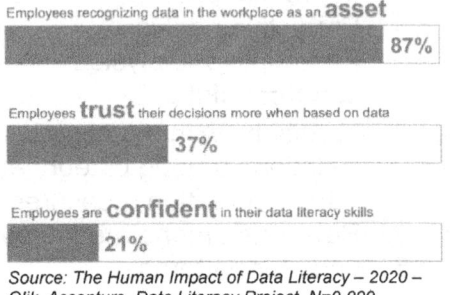

Source: The Human Impact of Data Literacy – 2020 – Qlik, Accenture, Data Literacy Project. N=9.000

We clearly have a challenge when it comes to our abilities to effectively use the data around us.

The training consists of four modules (3.5 hours per module). Two modules per training day (7 hours per ILT classroom).

We follow the four main components from the Data Literacy definition by MIT: Read data, Work with data, Analyze data and Argue with data.

We'll start with Read data, to learn and understand what data is and what aspects of the world it represents.

Next, we'll talk about Work with data, this involves creating, acquiring, cleaning, and managing data.

The second day we start with Analyze data. This is about using data to make informed decisions. Filtering, sorting, aggregating, comparing, and performing other analytical operations.

Finally, we wrap up this training with the module Argue with data: Using data to support a larger narrative intended to communicate some message to a particular audience.

3 Read Data

3.1 What is data?

Data itself is not reality, it reflects reality, like the plane in the water. It can represent and provide insights into various aspects of reality. Data is a representation of information gathered from observations, measurements, or records. It reflects events, phenomena, or processes that occur in the real world.

It's important to note that data is always subject to limitations and biases. The way data is collected, the selection criteria, and the interpretation can influence the insights derived from it. Therefore, while data can provide valuable information, it should be analyzed critically and in conjunction with other sources of knowledge to form a comprehensive understanding of reality. Keep in mind: all data is wrong (incomplete), but some data is useful.

Data can be defined as a collection of raw facts or figures that is typically represented in a quantitative or qualitative form. It refers to an object or an event that is collected, stored, and processed by various systems, tools, and technologies.

> Describes a *quality* or *quantity* of some *object* or *event*.

The value and significance of data lie in its potential to be analyzed, interpreted, and transformed into meaningful insights and knowledge. Analyzing data enables patterns, relationships, and trends to be identified, leading to informed decision-making and the discovery of new information. It allows us to capture and encode the properties of events and/or objects.

3.1.1 Data scales

Data can be defined as a collection of raw facts or figures that is typically represented in two types: a quantitative or a qualitative form.

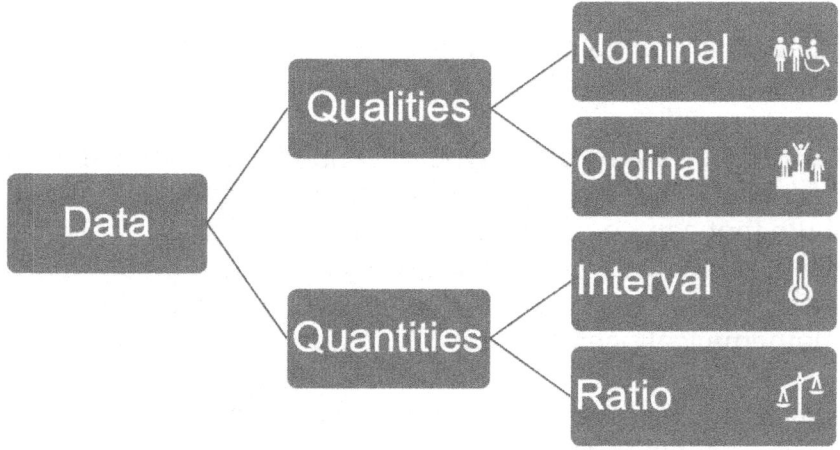

Qualitive data represents a set of distinct categories or groups that an observation or data point can belong to and can have the types: nominal or ordinal.

If we use a supermarket as an example:

Nominal variables represent categories without any inherent order or ranking. Like the color[1] of packaging (red, green, pink, yellow, or blue), the product packaging type (a box, a bag, or a bottle), product type (food vs. non-food), or the product brand name.

Ordinal variables have distinct categories with a specific order or ranking. The order represents a relative ranking but not necessarily the magnitude between categories. For instance, the NUTRI-SCORE (A, B, C, D or E, a nutrition label), shelf position (eye level=high attention), or for spicy food (Mild, Medium, Hot, Very Hot, Extremely Hot).

You can't calculate with these categories despite the order because it is impossible to tell the difference between the two ordered values. Let's take the spicy food example: How big or small is the gap between Hot food and Very Hot?

Qualitative values do not have a natural numerical order or magnitude, so you can't calculate with a qualitive value.

A **quantitative** variable is a type of variable that represents numerical quantities or measurements. It is a characteristic or attribute that can be measured on a numerical scale. Unlike qualitative variables, which represent categories or qualities, quantitative variables provide quantitative information and allow for mathematical operations and statistical analysis.

Quantitative variables can be further classified into two subtypes: interval & ratio.
It's important to note that while **interval** variables have a continuous nature, they **do not possess a true zero point**. This means that statements like "twice as much" or "half as much" do not hold any absolute meaning when referring to interval variables.

---

[1] Officially color does have a natural order (color spectrum), but most people don't use colors in this way. In practice you can use color as a nominal variable, but officially it is an ordinal variable.

Therefore, caution should be exercised when interpreting and making comparisons based on interval data. So, it lacks a true zero point and requires careful interpretation and consideration when making comparisons or drawing conclusions. Zero does not mean there is nothing!
Examples for interval are: the store location (longitude, latitude), the maximum temperature (in Celsius) to keep the product, the year of product production.

A **ratio** variable is a type of quantitative variable that possesses all the characteristics of an interval variable, with the additional property of having **a true zero point**. Zero means there is nothing!

It allows for meaningful ratios, proportions, and arithmetic operations. Ratio variables can be analyzed using a wide range of statistical techniques and enable precise comparisons and inferences.
Examples: The number of items on shelf, number of items in a pack, weight, price.

3.1.2 Why do we use data?
The purpose of data is to shed light on us and on our environment, to help us distinguish between truth and falsehood, and to enable us to choose sensible courses of action to take.

In one word, the chief goal of data is wisdom.

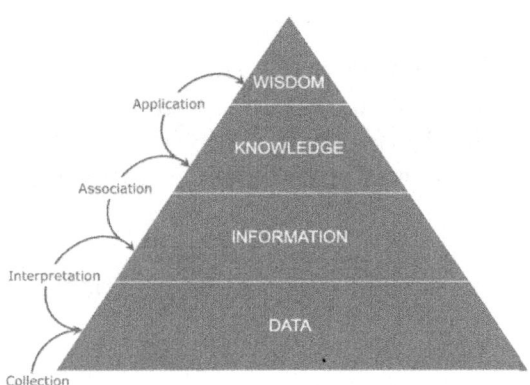

Source: Jones, Ben. *Data Literacy Fundamentals: Understanding the Power & Value of Data*

Data is the raw material, commonly (but not exclusively) in digital form, that allows us to capture and encode facts about our world.

Information is data that has been organized and formatted so that it's useful to us in some way. In other words, it's the shape and meaning of the data that turns it into information.

Information gets turned into **knowledge** when we incorporate it into our broader understanding of the world. We do this by linking the information we take in with other information, resulting in an accumulation of learning.

Learning is a matter of gathering knowledge; **Wisdom** is applying that knowledge.

We start with data collection, and then to turn that data into information we need to carry out accurate interpretation. And if we get from information to knowledge by making associations, then we get from knowledge to wisdom by correct application.

3.2 Summarize data

While averages provide valuable insights, it's important to note that they have limitations. They can be influenced by outliers, skewness in the data, or variations within subgroups.
Therefore, it's crucial to consider other statistical measures and explore the underlying data distribution for a comprehensive understanding.

Like this fictional example of Buena Vista City, Virginia:

Read Data

In Buena Vista City live 6,690 inhabitants. The total surface area is 16,9 square kilometers. The average income of Buena Vista City is $18,5K.

Suddenly, three men decide to buy new houses in Buena Vista City: LeBron James, Lionel Messi, and Tom Brady. The new inhabitant count of the city will be 6,690 + 3 = 6,693.

The average income is going to change too with these new inhabitants. The new average income will rise to $37K, meaning it doubles from the previous average!

This a typical case of outliers and skewness in the data: the average income is not an accurate representation of the income of the city, because our new inhabitants highly skew the data.

3.2.1 Central tendency
The measures of central tendency, which include the mean, median, and mode, describe different aspects of the distribution of a dataset. Here's how each measure is defined and what it reveals about the data:

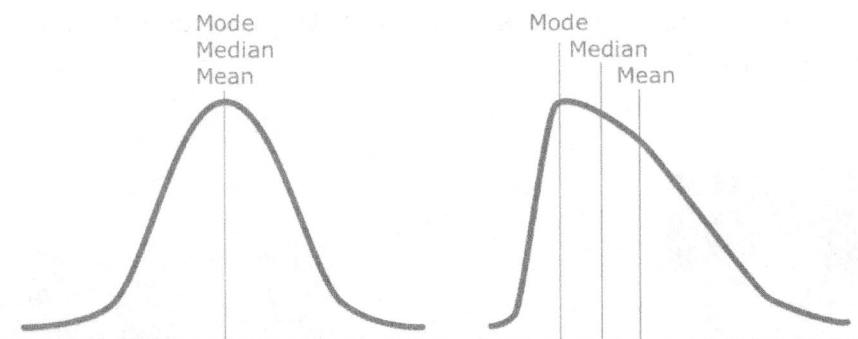

- **Mean**: The mean is calculated by adding up all the values in a dataset and dividing the sum by the total number of values. It represents the arithmetic average of the dataset. The mean is sensitive to extreme values or outliers because it considers every value in the dataset. It is commonly used when the data is normally distributed or symmetrically distributed.
Example:
Consider the dataset [2, 4, 6, 6, 8, 10].
- The mean is calculated as (2 + 4 + 6 + 6 + 8 + 10 = 36) / 6 = 6.
Consider the dataset [2, 4, 6, 6, 8, 100].
- The mean is calculated as (2 + 4 + 6 + 6 + 8 + 100 = 126) / 6 = 21.
- **Median**: The median is the middle value of an ordered dataset, separating the higher half from the lower half. To find the median, you arrange the values in ascending or descending order and identify the value in the middle. If the dataset has an even number of values, the median is the average of the two middle values. The median is not affected by extreme values and is useful when the data is skewed or contains outliers.
Example:
In the dataset [2, 4, 6, 6, 8, 10], the median is 6.
In the dataset [2, 4, 6, 6, 8, 100], the median is 6.
- **Mode**: The mode is the value or values that occur most frequently in a dataset. In other words, it represents the

most common value(s). A dataset can have no mode (when all values are unique), a single mode (when one value occurs more frequently than others), or multiple modes (when multiple values have the same highest frequency). The mode is useful for categorical or discrete data, but it can also be used with continuous data.
Example:
In the dataset [2, 4, 6, 6, 8, 10], the mode is 6 because it occurs twice, while other values occur only once.
In the dataset [2, 4, 6, 6, 8, 100], the mode is 6 because it occurs twice, while other values occur only once.

It's important to note that the choice of measure of central tendency depends on the nature of the data and the specific context of the analysis. Using multiple measures can provide a more comprehensive understanding of the data distribution and its characteristics.

3.2.2 How to summarize data
When we summarize data, we can't only look at a measure of central tendency (mean, median, mode). We also need consider two more characteristics of the data set.

To summarize a data set we need to consider all three of these data set characteristics:
- Measure of central tendency (mean, median, mode).
- Spread (lowest to highest and their distance, standard deviation, sigma, etc.).
- Shape of the data.

Source: Stephen S. Few, Now you see it, 2009

3.3 Consume data

The cognitive reflection test (CRT) is a task designed to measure a person's tendency to override an incorrect "gut" response and engage in further reflection to find a correct answer; however, the validity of the assessment as a measure of "cognitive reflection" or "intuitive thinking" is under question.

According to Shane Frederick, there are two general types of cognitive activity called "system 1" and "system 2" (these terms were first used by Keith Stanovich and Richard West). System 1 is executed quickly without reflection, while system 2 requires conscious thought and effort[2].

---

[2] Source: https://en.wikipedia.org/wiki/Cognitive_reflection_test

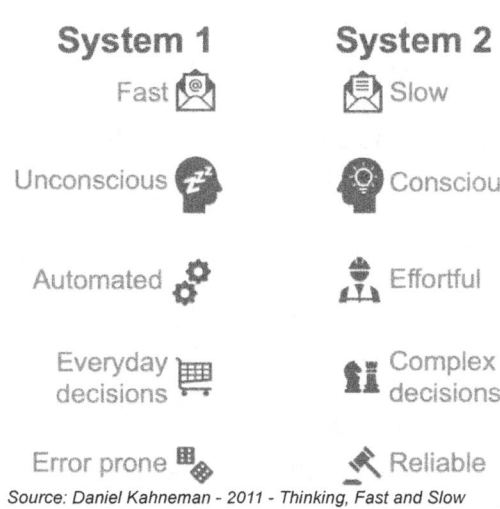

The cognitive reflection test has a question that has an obvious but incorrect response given by system 1. The correct response requires the activation of system 2. For system 2 to be activated, a person must note that their first answer is incorrect, which requires reflection on their own cognition.

Source: Daniel Kahneman - 2011 - Thinking, Fast and Slow

System 1: works automatically, unconscious, and fast, with little or no effort and no sense of control. Think of making simple everyday decisions like solving the sum 2+2, identifying the source of a particular sound, or driving a car on an empty road. This is your instinct.

System 2: involves conscious attention to the mental effort expended, making complicated calculations. We often link this system's functioning to subjective experience, choice, and concentration. Like making a complex and reliable decision for buying a new house, or like solving the sum 13 * 28, or comparing the price and quality ratio of a dishwasher. This is also called our analytical brain.

3.3.1 CHRTTS

Choosing the right chart for the right purpose is essential in data visualization because it directly impacts the effectiveness of conveying information, insights, and messages to your audience. Different types of charts are designed to represent specific types of data and patterns, and using the appropriate chart can make your data more accessible, understandable, and visually appealing. Here are some reasons why choosing the right chart is important:

1. **Clarity and communication**
   Each chart type has its strengths in presenting certain types of data. Using the right chart ensures that the data is presented in a clear and concise manner, making it easier for the audience to grasp the main points without confusion.
2. **Relevance and context**
   Different data visualization techniques provide different levels of detail and insight. Choosing the appropriate chart allows you to present the data in a way that is most relevant to your specific audience and context.
3. **Highlighting patterns and trends**
   Some charts are better at highlighting patterns and trends in data, such as line charts for time series data or scatter plots for correlations. Choosing the right chart enables you to emphasize the key insights effectively.
4. **Comparison**
   Certain charts, are excellent for comparing different categories or showing the composition of a whole. Selecting the right chart type helps you compare data points accurately.
5. **Avoiding misinterpretation**
   Using an inappropriate chart can lead to misinterpretation of data. For example, using a pie chart to represent many categories can make it hard to read and understand.

Read Data

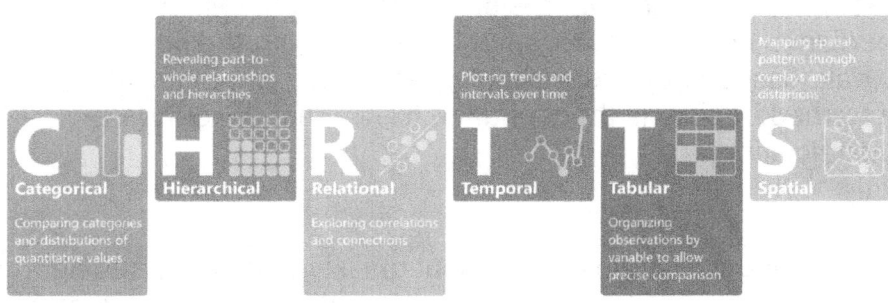

Based on: Data Visualization, Andy Kirk

To support the process of choosing the right visual, you could use the acronym CHRTTS and hereby some chart types per category:

- **Categorical**
  Bar chart, Column chart, Paired bar chart, Diverging bar chart, Dot plot, Marimekko, Isotype, Bullet chart, Bubble chart, Histogram, Pyramid chart, Strip plot, Box-and-whisker plot, Candlestick, Violin charts, Ridgeline plots, Raincloud, Stem and leaf plot, Bee swarm, Error-bars.
- **Hierarchy**
  Pie chart, Donut chart, Tree map, Stacked bar chart, Waffle chart, Waterfall chart, Parallel coordinates, Chord diagram, Sunburst.
- **Relationships**
  Scatter plot, Bubble chart, Merged bar chart, Heatmap, Sankey diagram.
- **Temporal**
  Line chart, Bump chart, Cycle plot, Area charts, Gantt, Stream graph, Connected scatter plot, Slope graph.
- **Tabular**
  Table, Matrix.
- **Spatial**
  Choropleth, Dot density map, Tile grid map, Cartograms, Proportional symbol map, Flow maps.

Selecting the right chart for your data visualization depends on the nature of your data, the story you want to tell, and the audience you are addressing. Understanding the strengths and weaknesses of different chart types allows you to make informed decisions that enhance the impact of your data visualization.

3.3.2 Categorical charts

Comparing categories is all about quickly and easily seeing the differences between the same values of different categories.

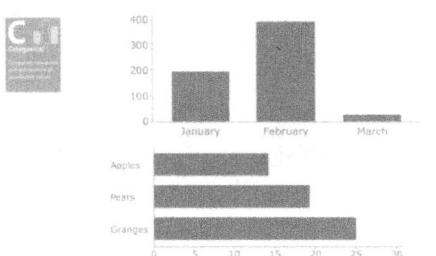

Bar charts are excellent for comparing data across different categories or groups. The length of the bars directly represents the values of the data points, making it easy to compare the magnitudes of different categories. Bar charts are ideal for representing discrete, categorical data, such as product categories, cities, months, or survey responses. Each category is represented by a separate bar, allowing you to display data for multiple categories side by side. They are simple and intuitive, making them easy for a wide range of audiences to understand. The clear visual representation of data values helps convey the main message quickly.

When you have data that can be ranked or ordered, bar charts allow you to present this information clearly. The order of the bars can represent the ranking or sorting of the categories, adding additional insights.

Bar charts are a valuable tool in the data visualization toolkit, particularly when dealing with categorical data and comparisons between different groups. By presenting data in a clear and concise manner, bar charts help audiences to understand the significance of the data and draw meaningful insights.

3.3.3 Hierarchical charts
Revealing part-to-whole relationships and hierarchies.

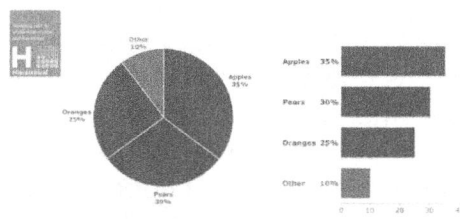

Part-to-whole: This kind of chart shows how the whole breaks up into constituent parts. A pie chart is the most common form for visualizing "part of a whole". There is much debate about the use of this form. This mainly concerns the degree of precision with which the data is presented. This has to do with the corners of the pie slices in combination with the round shape of a pie.

The great power of a pie chart is that the circle (the entire pie) represents 100% in its entirety. In addition, round shapes are often found more beautiful/attractive than straight shapes.

If we look at a pie chart, we translate its values by looking at the angle of a pie slice or the area of a pie slice.

If you are going to make or use pie charts, pay attention to these points:
1. Use a maximum of four pie slices. A pie chart remains legible if you limit the number of pie slices to a maximum of four pieces. If you have more categories, show the top three and add the remaining categories to the fourth (called Others).
2. Use one base color. Many different colors can be distracting so use one color and, if necessary, one other color to accentuate/emphasize a specific category. Then whiten the edges so that the pieces are clearly visible.
3. If possible (depending on the available space), put the labels and the values in the pie slices. This increases readability. With a legend next to the graph, the reader must read "back and forth". This is still possible with one chart, but if there are several, then it isn't very clear.

4. Refrain from using pie charts if you want to compare the pieces of a pie with the pieces in another pie. If you want to compare multiple values in a graph with other graphs, it is easier for the reader to compare by using a bar graph.
5. A reader compares the areas of the pieces (based on the angles). Consequently, it is intuitive to read a pie chart from top to bottom and then read it clockwise. Therefore, the ideal sorting of the pie pieces is to start at the top (at 12 o'clock) with the largest/most important point (clockwise). As a result, it is the first to receive the attention (it deserves). The other three pieces also start at 12 o'clock and then go counterclockwise in order of importance. The two most significant points are consequently at the top and are easy to compare because they have the same starting point, namely a vertical line. The two most minor important pieces will be placed where they will receive less attention. This ideal sorting is a bit more challenging in a software tool because you will have to sort the data (manually). If manual sorting is difficult or impossible, sorting from largest to smallest, starting at 12 o'clock, then going clockwise with the rest is the best method.

3.3.4 Relational charts

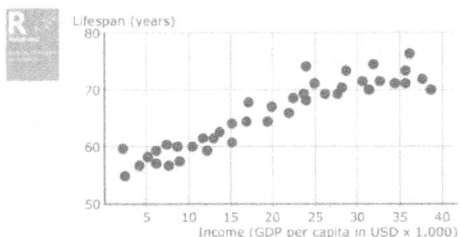

A scatter plot can be used to show a relationship between two (numerical) measured values. A point then represents each data point, and the horizontal (x-) axis contains the first value, and the vertical (y-) axis contains the second value. For example, if we want to show the relationship between age and salary for a department, then age is on the horizontal axis, and salary is on the vertical axis.

This is a compelling way to show the relationship, find outliers, detect clusters, or determine the general shape. The only thing you must pay attention to is the number of points that are shown. If these become too many, then the visualization can become difficult to read (overplotting). A popular way to address overplotting is by making the marks partially transparent.

3.3.5 Temporal charts

The line diagram is great to show change over time, or movement or flow in data. Because it concerns evolution, itis a perfect way to visualize a measurement value with intervals of (chronological) time. A straight line connects the different measurement values.

There are a few things to keep in mind when using a line chart:
1. **A line chart doesn't have to start at zero (like a bar chart)**
   Unlike the bar chart, the line chart does not have to start the y-axis on 0. The values in a line chart are based on the 2D position, and not on any length.
2. **Order the horizontal axis values from lowest to highest**
   When visualizing chronologically, it is easy for a reader to read if the time is ordered from lowest to highest. In the western world, we read from left to right, and if the axes are ordered similarly, it makes it easier to read.
3. **Don't use categories on the x-axis**
   The line chart only works if the x-axis variable has a clear order and fixed distance between the variable values.
4. **Always show all intervals**
   In addition to the previous point, do not omit gaps if there is no missing value! Always show all intervals in a

graph if there is a missing value or zero. A missing value is a strong signal that can't be simply ignored.

5. **Give the line some space**
   To show a clear comparison, it is good practice to keep the same amount of space both below the lowest value and above the highest value. To draw the line graph, use two-thirds of the area. Divide the remaining space above and below the graph.

6. **Watch out for the spaghetti effect**
   A line chart is a great way of comparing multiple categories in one visualization. However, too many lines (more than 5/6) can create a kind of spaghetti which makes it harder to read. An alternative is to use "small multiples" or several small graphs in which one specific category is highlighted in each graph through the use of color.

7. **Take the shortest route**
   Always draw the shortest line from point to point, so avoid using smoothed lines. Smoothing can obscure important details in the data and may lead to misinterpretations. Depending on the level of smoothing, it can either hide small-scale fluctuations or create false trends that do not exist in the actual data.

3.3.6 Tabular charts

	Jan	Feb	Mar	Apr	May	Jun
product 1	267	357	587	320	268	398
product 2	365	387	401	406	421	404
product 3	554	582	561	551	583	600
Total	1.186	1.326	1.549	1.277	1.272	1.402

	Jan	Feb	Mar	Apr	May	Jun
product 1	267	357	587	320	268	398
product 2	365	387	401	406	421	404
product 3	554	582	561	551	583	600
Total	1.186	1.326	1.549	1.277	1.272	1.402

It may not be the first thing that comes to mind when you think of data visualization, but the table is an essential basic shape. It is powerful in comparing (with great precision) individual values. The table also makes it possible to compare values of different units of measure (e.g., percentage of the total, average, amounts of money, numbers, etc.).

A matrix and a table visualization are both types of data representation used in data analysis. However, they differ in their purpose and layout.
- A matrix is a two-dimensional representation of data that is used to visualize the relationships between categories or dimensions (with a hierarchy). In a matrix visualization, the cells of the matrix represent the intersections between the rows and columns, and the values in the cells can be used to represent a variety of measures, such as counts, sums, or averages. Matrix visualizations are typically used to highlight patterns and trends in large data sets. Great for human consumption.
- A table is a simple arrangement of data in rows and columns, where each row represents an observation, and each column represents a field or attribute of that observation. Tables are used to display detailed information about individual observations and to compare different attributes side by side.

3.3.7 Spatial charts

If physical location is an essential factor (geographical), maps are a good tool. Using maps, the data is enriched with position and distance between places.

Here you have two European countries highlighted with the RED color: Andorra (between Spain and France) and Turkey. Which draws more attention?
Turkey, because it is bigger, so there are more red pixels.
Question is: does area play a role in our analysis?

The size of an area (here, a country) doesn't have to be related to the value shown with the color intensity (for example the number of patients). In other words, a large country seems to have a greater value because it uses a larger surface area of

the visualization. But the area says nothing about the measured value that is displayed.
Applying a map in this way only indicates the values' geographical distribution. So usually, this shape is complemented by another visualization to add precision. It is also a good tool for identifying exceptions. Most people have no logical order in colors, so there are better options than using different colors. It is best to use only one color and use a dark variant for high values and a lighter variant for lower values

3.4 Check your data

Whenever you are exposed to data it is good to ask yourself the following eight questions:

- Why does the data matter to you?
- Does the claim match the data?
- Does the claim seem plausible?
- What comparison needs to be made?
- Who's saying it?
- How was the data gathered?
- What's missing?
- Is the data being distorted?

Based on: https://www.geckoboard.com/best-practice/data-claim-checklist/

1. **Why does the data matter to you?**
   First you need to determine if the data makes you happy or sad. If you feel emotional about the data, it is best to find help from others. Ask others to explain what they conclude from the data. Whenever we feel emotional about data, we tend to fall into the traps of biases (confirmation bias).
2. **Does the claim match the data?**
   Is the headline misleading? Has the data been over-simplified, over-inflated, or otherwise dramatized to become a sensational headline?
   Has a generalization been made that doesn't accurately

reflect the data?

What's the small print? Headlines often omit key details. Real life example: A 2013 Times article claimed, "More people have cell phones than toilets." However, by looking at the actual data, we find that more people have access to mobile phones than toilets. "Access" is a tricky word because it could mean that dozens of people share a single mobile phone, but the Times headline makes it sound like the number of cell phones exceeds the number of toilets.

3. **Does the claim seem plausible?**
Perform a sanity check of the claim. Do some quick back-of-the-envelope math or use your own prior knowledge. Are there other, more plausible explanations for the effect? Could they have made a mistake?
Can you verify the claim in any other way? Perhaps you have access to other data or can pull a report from another source.
The less plausible the claim, the more heavily you'll want to scrutinize everything else.
Real life example: You're a customer support rep and your boss claims that "Our best customer support rep can resolve 800 tickets via phone a day." Let's do some quick math to see if this is plausible.
5 seconds (answer the phone and get the customer's name)
5 seconds (pull up customer's account and ask what the problem is)
10 seconds (customer explains the problem)
30 seconds (verify the problem or find the source)
40 seconds (fix the problem)
= 90 seconds per ticket or 40 tickets per hour

4. **What comparison needs to be made?**
Data is all about "compared to what?" Last week? Last year? Competitor(s)? Revenue?
Real life example: Several years ago, Colgate ran an advertising campaign claiming that "80% of dentists recommend Colgate." The implied comparison is that

dentists recommend Colgate over and above other brands. However, the Advertising Standards Authority discovered that in the survey, dentists could recommend more than one toothpaste. In fact, another competitor was recommended almost as often as Colgate was.

5. **Who's saying it?**
   Are they an expert?
   What is their agenda? Combined with the plausibility of the claim, this will affect how heavily you'll need to scrutinize the data.
   Where did the data come from in the first place?
   Real life example: In 1998, a research paper published in The Lancet claimed there was a link between certain vaccines and Autism. Several subsequent studies by independent organizations showed the author of the paper, Andrew Wakefield, manipulated the evidence to create the appearance of a link in his research. Although he was a gastroenterologist and medical researcher, he wasn't an expert in toxicology, genetics, neurology, or other disciplines necessary to be an expert on autism. Additionally, he failed to disclose a conflict of interest as he received significant money to prove the vaccine was dangerous.

6. **How was the data gathered?**
   How did they arrive at their conclusion/claim?
   Often it's not that easy to gather the exact data you need/want. What was their methodology? Have any approximations been made? Were these done sensibly? Is there too much extrapolation? Were best practices followed (such as significance tests, sampling biases avoided, etc.)?
   Example: Suppose you want to know how long it takes a cup of coffee (at 140 degrees Fahrenheit) to cool to room temperature. After observing for three minutes, you find the coffee cools by five degrees every minute.
   If you then extrapolate that data (extending the trend of five degrees cooler per minute), you could end up with the ridiculous conclusion that after 30 minutes, the

coffee would freeze.
This extrapolation fails to consider physical limits (coffee cannot become colder than room temperature) and that the rate of cooling slows as it gets closer to room temperature.

7. **What's missing?**
Was their sample representative of the whole?
Has the data been "cherry picked" (i.e., only using the information that they want)?
Do you have other data that would help put the claim into context?
Real life example: Global warming is an often-debated topic where both "sides" have trends to back their claims. This is achieved by cherry picking only the data that supports their position, while omitting the rest.

8. **Is the data being distorted?**
In addition to cherry picking, other tactics might be employed. For example, the line chart axis might be cropped, or a misleading average might be shown.
Real life example: In 2012, Fox Business showed a chart visualizing the impact if Bush tax cuts were to expire. The top tax rate would change from 35% to 39.6%. However, the axis was cropped - beginning at 34% instead of 0% which made the tax increase appear larger than it actually was.

4 Work With Data

4.1 Creating data

Data can be created through a variety of methods, including automated and manual processes.

4.1.1 Automated data

Automated data creation typically involves the use of technology such as sensors, scanners, or software programs that collect and process data automatically without human intervention.

For example, a website may automatically track user behavior and generate data about which pages are visited and how long users stay on each page. Similarly, a manufacturing plant may use sensors to collect data about the temperature, pressure, and other variables in its production process.

A sensor is set up to detect certain activities or conditions. A lot of assumptions are often made about the conditions under which the data is collected, so this can go terribly wrong if those conditions change.

4.1.2 Manual data

On the other hand, manual data creation involves humans actively collecting and entering data into a system. This can be done through a variety of methods such as surveys, interviews, or manual data entry. For example, a marketing research firm may conduct a survey to collect data about customer preferences, or a government agency may collect census data through door-to-door surveys.

It's important to note that data creation methods can also be a combination of automated and manual processes. For instance, an online retailer may use automated software to track sales data but also employ human data analysts to interpret the data and make recommendations for business strategy.

People might say that a lot can go wrong with this method of data entry; that is true, we humans are very good at approximations. On the other hand, the advantage is that people can deal flexibly with changing circumstances (emergence of mobile numbers instead of fax numbers).

4.2 Data quality

Often, we use the following (practical) definition of data quality: *"Data is of high quality if the data is fit for the intended purpose."*

But what happens when the purpose changes? Or if you want to use the data more broadly? Like:

You have addresses collected to send letters to, and now you want to visit the address... But what if the collected address is a PO box?

What is a customer in your organization? A customer may be slightly different in the Finance department (payer) than in the Sales department (decision maker).

There is also another definition of data quality: *"Data is of high quality if the data correctly represents the real-world construct that the data describes."*

This is an ideal picture, but it is virtually unattainable. It requires data to represent reality perfectly. And this is never the case.

4.2.1 Data quality dimensions

A data quality dimension is a measurable aspect or characteristic of data. The word dimension appeals to the idea that the quality of data can be assessed by looking at different characteristics of the data. There are endless lists of data quality dimensions and a full overview can't be given.

Therefore, we will only cover a short list with dimensions that are frequently used in practice:

- **Completeness**
  Data is considered "complete" when it fulfils expectations of comprehensiveness. Let's say that you ask the customer to supply his or her name. You might make a customer's middle name optional, but if you have the first and last name, the data is complete.
  There are things you can do to improve this data quality dimension. You'll want to assess whether all the requisite information is available, and whether there are any missing elements.

- **Timeliness**
  Is your information available at the point it's needed? That data quality dimension is called "timeliness." Let's say that you need financial information every quarter; if the data is ready when it's supposed to be, it's timely.
  The data quality dimension of timeliness is a user expectation. If your information isn't ready exactly when you need it, it doesn't fulfil that dimension.

- **Uniqueness**
  "Unique" information means that there's only one instance of it appearing in a database. As we know, data duplication is a frequent occurrence. "Daniel A. Robertson" and "Dan A. Robertson" may well be the same person.
  Meeting this data quality dimension involves reviewing your information to ensure that none of it is duplicated.

- **Consistency**
  At many companies, the same information may be stored in more than one place. If that information matches, it's considered "consistent." For example, if your human resources information systems say an employee doesn't work there anymore, yet your payroll says he's still receiving a check, that's inconsistent.
  To resolve issues with inconsistency, review your data sets to see if they're the same in every instance. Are there any instances in which the information conflicts with itself?

- **Accuracy**
  The term "accuracy" refers to the degree to which information accurately reflects an event or object described. For example, if a customer's age is 32, but the system says she's 34, that information is inaccurate.
  What steps can you take to improve your accuracy? Ask yourself whether the information represents the reality of the situation. Is there incorrect data (that needs to be fixed)?

4.2.2 Avoid confusing data

As we have seen before, data can be confusing. Data is merely a representation of reality, so make sure not to confuse it with actual reality. Often, we receive data from others or share it with others. There are some pitfalls to consider in preventing confusing data.

- **Clearly understand the operational definitions of all metrics**
  Make sure definitions of metrics are clear. For example, what does it mean when you count a "customer"? Is a customer somebody who visits your store, or is a customer someone who actually makes a purchase?
- **Draw the data collection steps as a process flow diagram**
- A process flow diagram greatly increases the understanding of how and when data is collected, helping you to place it in the correct context.**Understand the limitations and inaccuracies of each step in the process**
  In every step of the data collection or processing process there may be limitations or inaccuracies. For example, if you are manually counting traffic at a certain road, you may miss some counts during lunch or at night.
- **Identify any changes in method or equipment over time**
  Changing your method or equipment can introduce unwanted variances in your data. For instance, changing

to another temperature sensor or placing it at a different location can greatly influence your temperature read outs.
- **Seek to understand the motives of the people collecting and reporting**
Understanding why data was collected or reported can make you aware of potential biases or incentives. If someone is trying to support an argument with data, the chances are that the data collected is not as objective as we would hope.
- **Visualize the data and investigate any shifts, outliers, and trends for possible discrepancies**
Visualizing your data and looking through it is a great way to discover shifts, outliers, and trends in your data. Observing and thinking critically is one of your greatest assets in assessing data quality.

4.3 Acquiring & cleaning data

After the data has been collected, there are steps you must take to be able to analyze it effectively. Your raw data must be converted into appropriate file types, and the various data types must be normalized. For example, if you want to compare strings at some point, then make sure to use capitals and accents consequently over all strings. A similar example is the registration of dates: make sure they are all written in the same way, such as 04-10-2023 or 20231004. Choose a format and stick with it.

Make sure your data is valid, by checking for missing values and understanding where they come from. Also, check for implausible values (a negative price of a product would be unlikely) and implausible combinations (LeBron James becomes a member of the Rolling Stones).

4.3.1 Tidy data

Source: Tidy Data – Hadley Wickham 2014

During the step to make data valid, we also must deal with incorrect structure.
There is one data structure that works well with all reporting/analysis tools: tidy data (aka Star Schema).

Tidy data is a concept introduced by statistician Hadley Wickham that refers to a specific data organization and formatting paradigm designed to simplify data analysis and manipulation.

The principles of tidy data aim to create a consistent and structured data representation that allows for straightforward data analysis and visualization.

Tidy data is a standard way of mapping the meaning of a dataset to its structure. A dataset is messy or tidy depending on how rows, columns and tables are matched up with observations, variables and types.

In tidy data:
- Each variable forms a column.
- Each observation forms a row.
- Each type of observational unit forms a table.

4.3.2 Combine data

Our data is cleaned, wrangled and we are now ready to connect or join the data. For combining data, we have roughly two options: joining and appending the data.

Inner join

An inner join is a type of join operation in a relational database that combines rows from two or more tables based on a matching condition and produces a result set that contains only the rows where the join condition is satisfied.

More specifically, an inner join returns only the rows from both tables that have matching values in the specified column(s). Any rows in either table that do not have a match in the other table are not included in the result set.

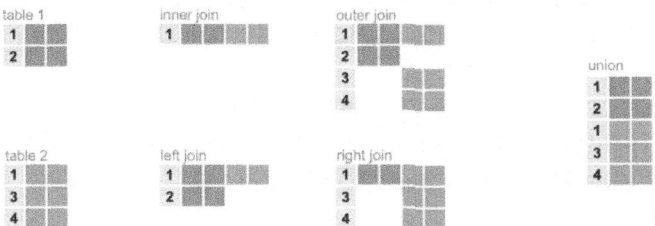

- **Outer join**

An outer join is a type of join operation in a relational database that combines rows from two or more tables based on a matching condition and produces a result set that includes all the rows from one or both tables, along with any unmatched rows. This join returns all the rows from both tables and includes null values for any columns that do not have a matching row in the other table.

- **Left join**

A left join (also known as a left outer join) combines rows from two or more tables based on a matching condition and produces a result set that includes all the rows from the left table, along with any matching rows from the right table. If there is no matching row in the right table, the result set contains null values for the right table's columns.

In a left join, the left table is the "primary" table, and its rows are all included in the result set. Only the matching rows from the right table are included in the result set, along with any null values for its columns in the non-matching rows.

- **Right join**

A right join (also known as a right outer join) is the opposite of the left join. Now, the right table is the "primary" table. The result set will therefore contain all rows from the right table, along with matching rows from the left table.

- **Union**

A union, or append, is an operation in which multiple tables are appended to each other. For a successful union, the tables must adhere to the following requirements:
1. The number of columns must be the same for all tables.
2. The columns must be of compatible data types.

In some cases, the union operation automatically removes duplicate records. Make sure you are aware of this setting when appending your data.

4.4 Managing data

Data requires management.

More and more individuals become responsible for managing their own data. They're made responsible for managing local data sets, reports, and dashboards. However, managing data and reports is not just about the data itself. It's

> *Data management is about **people, processes**, and **technology**, in that order.*

about people, processes, and technology. These three factors all play an important role in the successful management of data.

Without properly managing our data people will stop using it, because:
- They can't rely on the quality.
- Re-use becomes difficult.
- Data becomes corrupted.
- Data is located somewhere, but it is not clear where.

4.4.1 KPI mantras
When it comes to controlling our processes, the most important type of data (information) that we encounter every day is the KPI: Key Performance Indicator.
This is a definition of a KPI: "*A way to measure how something or someone is doing.*"

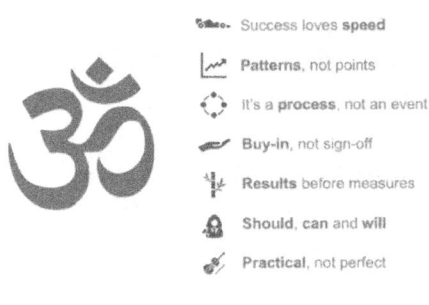

- Success loves **speed**
- **Patterns**, not points
- It's a **process**, not an event
- **Buy-in**, not sign-off
- **Results** before measures
- **Should**, can and will
- **Practical**, not perfect

Source: Stacey Barr, PuMP

However, it may be better to leave "someone" out here, because:
- If you start measuring people, you will only get disappointments and frustrations!
- When measuring people, you will get the result you ask for. But is this the result you need?

Here we have the seven KPI mantras from the PuMP approach to performance management and KPI's by Stacey Barr. PuMP is a practical and engaging performance measurement approach to developing KPIs that are meaningful and measure what matters:

1. **Success loves speed.**
   It means that the faster you move, the faster you fail; the faster you fail, the faster you learn; and the faster you learn, the faster you succeed. Don't waste time over-planning. Do more action-learning.
2. **Patterns, not points.**
   Often I'll add a second part to this one: "Signals, not noise." It's about our obsession with comparing this month's performance to last month, or the same month last year. How do you know last month, or the same month last year were normal? Two points of data do not contain any signals about whether something has changed. We need to look for patterns in our performance measures' time series, because that's where we'll find the true signals.
3. **It's a process, not an event.**
   Performance measurement is not a brainstorming session squeezed into the last day of the annual planning workshop. Treating it as an event like this causes most of the problems we have with measurement. No, performance measurement is a process, a series of steps that involve selecting meaningful measures, bringing them to life usefully, and then using them to guide decisions about performance improvement.
4. **Buy-in, not sign-off.**
   Buy-in is when someone has been involved in helping to create something. When you do that, you invest some of yourself in that thing. It's the same for performance measures: when people help create them, they feel a stronger sense of owning them. That's the way to get people engaged in bringing measures to life and using them to improve performance. Sign-off doesn't even come close.
5. **Results before measures.**
   "So, what should our measures be?" Wrong question. The right question is "So, what results are important for us to achieve?" Then you should ask "How will we

recognize those results happening?", and thusly "What are some sensible ways to measure those results?". Measure design is a deliberate procedure, not a creative brainstorming session.

6. **Should, can and will.**
   How many measures should you have? I don't know. But I do know that the only results worth measuring are those that you should, can and will do something about. If it's not an important performance result, then you shouldn't do anything about it. If it's a result outside your circle of influence, then you can't do anything about it. If you just don't feel the passion for it or haven't got the time for it, then you won't do anything about it.

7. **Practical, not perfect.**
   One of the biggest delays in the flow of the performance measurement process is procrastination. We procrastinate on choosing measures because our goals aren't yet clear enough. We procrastinate on performance reporting because our measures aren't spot-on yet. We procrastinate on performance improvement because the measures aren't complete enough or accurate enough. Some information is better than no information. And success loves speed.

5 Analyze Data

Analysis is a detailed examination of anything complex to understand its nature or to determine its essential features: a thorough study.

5.1 Expectations

Before starting to analyze data, take a step back and consider these two questions:
1. What do I expect to see, find? Translate this into a hypothesis, and then focus on rejecting this hypothesis.
2. What would I like to see, find? This helps in identifying a potential bias towards the analysis.

5.2 Thinking shortcuts

Being aware of our biases before starting an analysis is essential for maintaining objectivity, ensuring accurate results, enhancing credibility, and promoting fairness and ethical conduct. It ultimately improves the quality of our work and decision-making processes.

The two types of shortcuts in our thinking are cognitive bias and logical fallacies.

Cognitive bias is a systematic thought process caused by the tendency of the human brain to simplify information processing through a filter of personal experience and preferences. The filtering process is a coping mechanism that enables the brain to prioritize and process large amounts of information quickly.

Simplification helps make things more accessible, understandable, and efficient. However, there's a critical caveat: one should not oversimplify to the point of losing essential details or accuracy. Oversimplification can lead to misrepresentation, misunderstanding, or inaccurate conclusions. There are situations where complexities are inherent and necessary to capture the full scope of a problem or concept. The goal is to simplify and distill information to its essential components without sacrificing accuracy or relevance.

Logical fallacies are flaws in an argument that weaken the argument or make the conclusion invalid. They can be unintentional mistakes or deliberate attempts to deceive or manipulate the audience. Understanding logical fallacies allows us to identify weak or deceptive arguments and strengthens our ability to construct and evaluate well-reasoned and valid arguments.

The **Cognitive Bias Codex** is a visual tool that organizes biases in a meaningful way. It is broken down into four main categories:

- Too much information.
- Not enough meaning.
- Need to act fast.
- What should we remember.

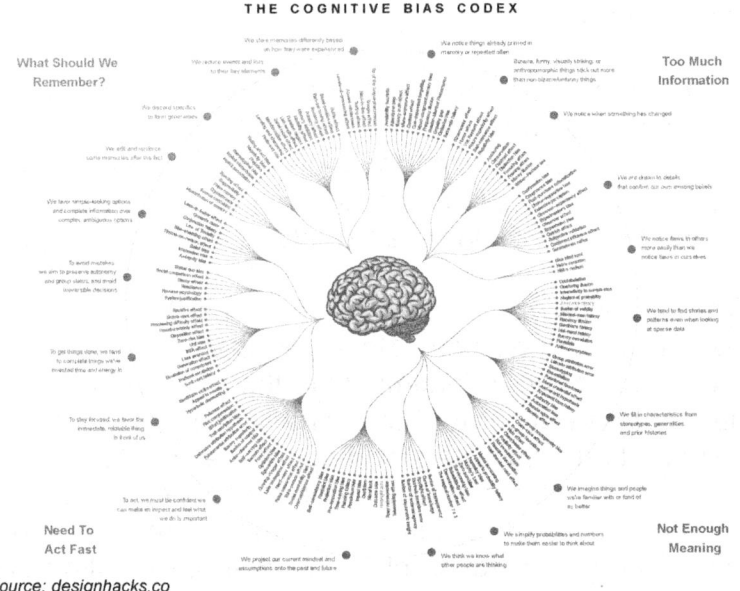

Source: designhacks.co

5.2.1 Confirmation bias
Confirmation bias refers to the tendency of people to only pay attention to information that agrees with what they already believe and ignore information that disagrees with this.

In the scientific method, addressing confirmation bias is crucial. Scientists aim to approach research with an objective mindset, seeking evidence that either supports or refutes a hypothesis. The peer-review process and replication studies help minimize the impact of confirmation bias and promote the advancement of knowledge through rigorous examination of evidence.

5.2.2 Survivorship bias
Survivorship bias refers to the tendency to focus only on what succeeded or survived, while ignoring what failed or didn't survive. This bias can be seen in various contexts, such as historical analysis, business decision-making, or self-improvement.

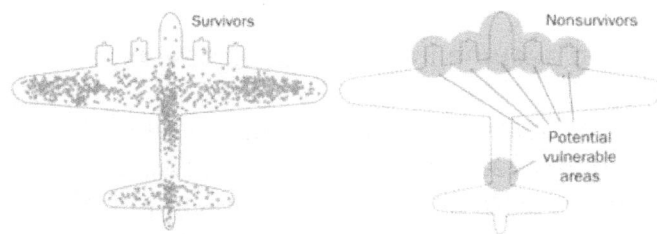

Source: https://en.wikipedia.org/wiki/Survivorship_bias

This figure shows a hypothetical pattern of damage to planes with which they could still return home. If the aircraft was reinforced in the most commonly hit areas, this would be a result of survivorship bias because crucial data from fatally damaged planes was being ignored; those hit in other places did not survive.

5.2.3 Curse of knowledge
The tendency to assume other people have the necessary context or knowledge to follow what you're communicating is

referred to as the Curse of Knowledge. As a result, you might use complex language, technical jargon, or make references that are unfamiliar to the audience, making it difficult for others to grasp the information.

By being mindful of the curse of knowledge, individuals can become better communicators and educators, fostering more effective and inclusive interactions with others regardless of their level of expertise.

5.2.4 Correlation vs causation

Correlation is about how two variables are related: when one variable changes, the other tends to change too. If the variables are positively correlated, they both increase or decrease together. If they are negatively correlated, as one variable goes up, the other goes down, and vice versa. It's important to remember that correlation doesn't mean there is a cause-and-effect relationship between the variables. It only shows that there is an association between them.

By default, we need to assume there is NO causation.

Causality, on the other hand, is about a cause-and-effect relationship between two variables. In a causal relationship, changes in one variable directly lead to changes in the other. Proving causality goes beyond just finding a correlation. It requires strong evidence that shows how one variable influences the other, while also ruling out the possibility of other factors or coincidences causing the observed relationship.

By being mindful of the correlation-causation fallacy and adopting critical thinking, individuals can avoid making erroneous assumptions and better understand the complex relationships between variables in scientific research and everyday life.

5.3 Types of analysis

Numerous types of analysis exist, each suited to different purposes and fields of study. These are five common types of data analysis, but many others exist:

1) Descriptive – what happened?
2) Diagnostic – what is going on under the surface?
3) Inferential – what about the rest of the population?
4) Predictive – what is likely to happen next?
5) Prescriptive – what should we do about it?

5.3.1 Descriptive analysis

Descriptive analysis answers the question: What has happened? It is used to describe and summarize a set of data to gain insights into its main characteristics. It involves organizing, describing, and visualizing data to understand its distribution, central tendency, variability, and other essential features. The primary purpose of descriptive analysis is to describe and provide a comprehensive overview of the data.

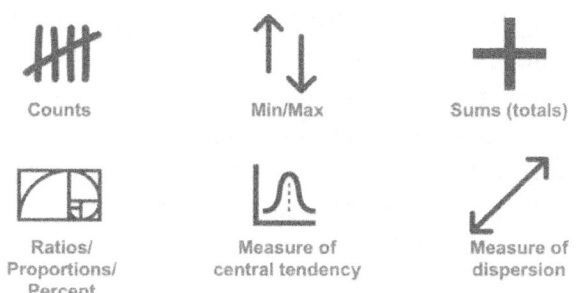

Descriptive analysis involves the use of statistical measures such as mean, median, mode, standard deviation, range, and frequency distribution to describe the data. These measures provide a way to understand the central tendency, variability, and distribution of the data.

5.3.2 Diagnostic analysis

Diagnostic analysis is a type of data analysis that focuses on understanding the reasons behind specific outcomes or events. It goes beyond  descriptive analysis, which only provides a summary of data. It aims to identify the underlying causes or factors that contribute to specific observations or a problem or issue. The primary purpose of diagnostic analysis is to answer the "why" questions and gain insights into the root causes of problems or successes, undertaken through activities such as drilling down, finding correlations, and spotting outliers.

Examples of diagnostic analysis include:
- Investigating why sales declined in a specific region or during a particular period.
- Identifying the factors that contribute to customer churn in a subscription-based service.
- Understanding the reasons behind an increase in employee turnover in a company.
- Analyzing the impact of marketing campaigns on website traffic and conversion rates.

5.3.3 Inferential analysis

Inferential analysis is an analysis technique used to draw conclusions about a population based on a sample of data. It involves utilizing probability theory and statistical models to estimate or predict the characteristics of a population based on samples and can be used to make predictions, test hypotheses, and draw conclusions about that population. It is

important to note that
the validity of the
conclusions drawn from
inferential analysis
depends on the quality
of the sample(s) and
the appropriateness of
the statistical
techniques used.

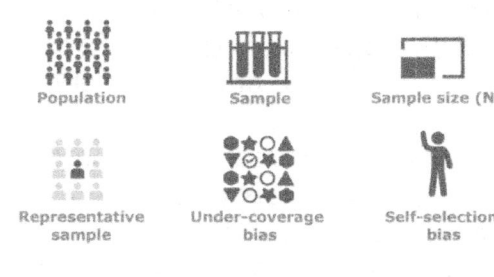

The main concepts in inferential analysis are:
- **Population**
Any group of individual members that have at least one trait in common.
- **Sample**
A smaller number of observations taken from the total that makes up the population.
- **Sample size** (N)
The number of observations taken from the population.
- **Representative samples**
A representative sample is a subset of a population that seeks to accurately reflect the characteristics of the larger group. It can be used for obtaining insights and observations about a targeted population group.
- **Under-coverage bias**
Under-coverage bias occurs when a part of the population is excluded from your sample. As a result, the sample is no longer representative of the target population.
- **Self-selection bias**
Self-selection bias occurs when the decision to participate in a study is left entirely up to individuals. This gives rise to research bias because those who volunteer to take part in research studies are usually different from those who don't (e.g., in terms of motivation or demographics).

5.3.4 Predictive analysis
Predictive analysis is a statistical analysis technique that uses data, statistical algorithms, and machine learning models to

make predictions about future events or behavior. The goal of predictive analysis is to identify patterns in historical data and use them to make predictions about future outcomes.

Common techniques used in predictive analysis are:
- **(Linear) Regression**

Regression is a statistical method that attempts to determine the relationship between a dependent variable and a series of other variables (known as independent variables).
- **Pattern recognition**

With pattern recognition, we aim to use machine learning algorithms to automatically recognize patterns and regularities in data.

With these techniques, we can make predictions about future events. It is important to approach predictions with caution and an understanding of the limitations of the data and the method you're using. Error margins help us make more informed decisions and set realistic expectations about the accuracy of our forecasts.

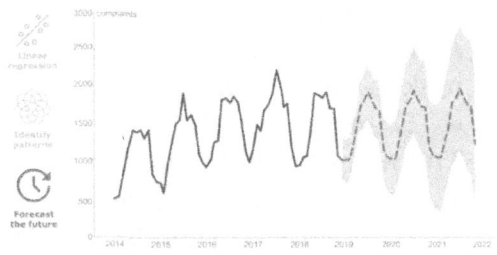

Source: Jones, Ben. *Data Literacy Fundamentals: Understanding the Power & Value of Data*

5.3.5 Prescriptive analysis

Prescriptive analysis is an advanced data analysis technique that uses mathematical algorithms, machine learning models, and optimization techniques to provide recommendations or actions that can be taken to optimize a process or outcome. The goal of prescriptive analysis is to identify the best course of action among various options to achieve a desired outcome.

Source: https://blog.griddynamics.com/customer-churn-prevention-prescriptive-solution-using-deep-learning/ & https://kpi-max.com/churn-rate/

Prescriptive analysis is considered the most advanced and complex type of data analysis and requires significant expertise in mathematics, computer science, and statistics.

5.4 Analytical skills

Thorough analysis is based on a solid understanding of the underlying data.

Context is essential when using data because it helps to ensure that the data is correctly interpreted and analyzed. Without context, data can be misinterpreted, leading to incorrect conclusions and decisions.

Here are some reasons why context is important when using data:

- **Helps to understand the data:** Context provides background information that helps to understand what

the data is and how it was collected. This information can help to determine the accuracy and reliability of the data.
- **Enables appropriate analysis:** Context helps to determine the appropriate methods of analysis for the data. For example, if the data is from a survey, it may be necessary to weight the data to adjust for sampling biases.
- **Helps to identify trends:** Context helps to identify trends and patterns in the data. Understanding the context in which the data was collected can help to explain why certain trends are present.
- **Enables comparisons:** Context enables comparisons to be made between different data sets. Without context, it can be difficult to determine whether two data sets are comparable.
- **Reduces errors:** Context helps to reduce errors in data analysis by providing a framework for interpreting the data. When context is absent, there is a greater risk of errors due to misinterpretation.

We will now zoom into the analysis of qualitative and quantitative data. Instead of using terms like "quality" or "quantity," software tools often adopt the terms "category" and "measure," respectively.

 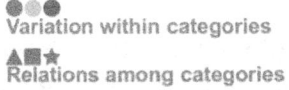 Variation within measures
Relations among measures

Source: S. Few – Signal

5.4.1 Variations within categories

For the analysis of variations within categories, we often use the following operations: tallying, summation, averaging, ranking and part-to-whole. We usually need a numerical value to summarize the data (such as revenue for a given product).

5.4.2 Relations among categories

Tables are a great way to study the relationship between categories. You just show the actual data and let the reader figure relations out. However, it may take quite some effort to compare proportions and patterns. A solution to this is to visualize the values using bars. This way the reader can easily spot relations between categories.

5.4.3 Variations within measures

When looking for variations within measures, we are often interested in finding signals. These can be sudden changes over time, periodicity, a trend, the lack of change over time, etc.

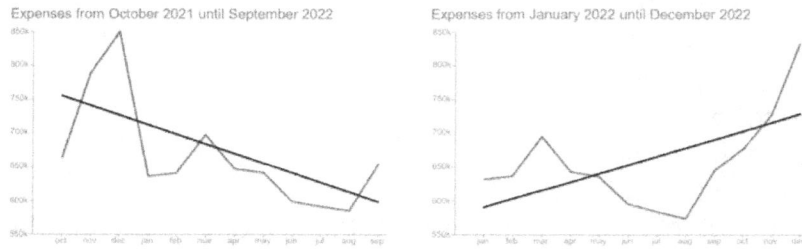

Often a trend line is incorporated when showing data over time. However, the timeframe on which the trend line is based may significantly affect the slope of the trend.

An alternative to a trend line can be a moving average. While it may be less straightforward than a trend line (up or down), it provides a better representation of the development of these values over time.

When dealing with
periodic patterns in
data, a trend line or
moving average may
not capture the relevant
signals in the data.
Instead, a cycle plot
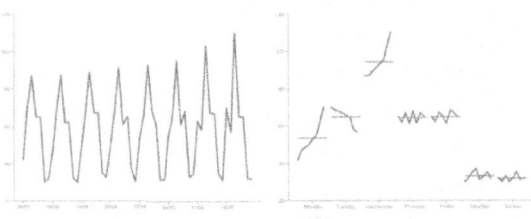
may prove useful. With a cycle plot, we visualize how a trend,
or a cycle correlated with the day-of-the-week, or the month-of-
the-year evolves. A cycle plot is made to capture visually how
certain values have advanced over a period.

5.4.4 Relations among measures
Two variables correlate when the variation in one variable
systematically moves with the other.

Correlation: Correlation
refers to the statistical
relationship between
two variables. When two
variables are correlated,
their values tend to
move together
predictably. If one
variable increases, the
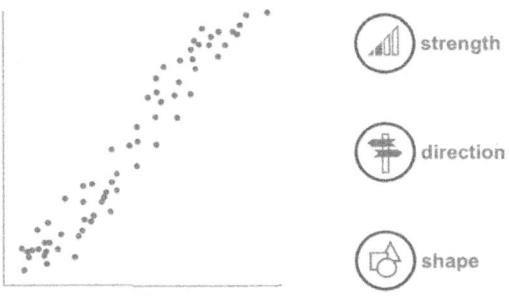
other might increase (positive correlation), or if one variable
increases, the other might decrease (negative correlation).

Strength of correlation: The strength of correlation indicates
how closely the two variables are related. It is represented by a
correlation coefficient, which ranges between -1 and +1. A
correlation coefficient of +1 indicates a perfect positive
correlation (both variables move in the same direction with a
constant ratio); meanwhile -1 shows a perfect negative
correlation (both variables move in opposite directions with a
constant ratio), and 0 indicates no correlation (no systematic
relationship between the variables).

Direction of correlation: The direction of correlation determines the nature of the relationship between the variables. A positive correlation means that as one variable increases, the other also tends to increase. On the other hand, a negative correlation means that as one variable increases, the other tends to decrease.

Form of correlation: Correlation refers to the pattern of data points plotted on a graph. It can be classified as either linear or non-linear. In a linear correlation, the data points form a straight line when plotted on a scatter plot. In a non-linear correlation, the data points follow a more complex pattern, such as creating clusters, curves, or gaps.

5.4.5 Look for patterns

To convey the message of your data analysis, you can use one or more of the following story points:

Change over time focuses on how a metric shifts over time. For example, you might highlight how there's a downward or upward trend in a key metric (gradual or sharp). Even no change in a trended line may be a story point when something was expected to happen. For example, your company's investment in safety training doesn't reduce the workplace injury rate.

Relationship highlights how two things are related to each other in some way. You may show how there is a positive or negative correlation between two metrics that may or may not imply causation. For example, you could show how higher customer satisfaction scores may be contributing to a higher customer renewal rate.

Intersection reveals the moment when one metric surpasses or falls below another metric (or the same thing happens between two plotted values). When one metric intersects with another, it could be a positive or negative sign depending on the situation. For example, you may be highlighting when your start-up's revenues surpassed costs (finally profitable), or when revenues fell below costs, indicating you still have operational issues to address.

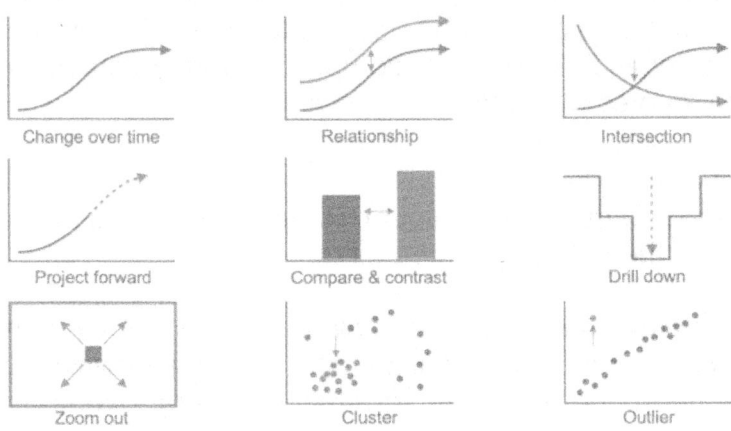

Source: Brent Dykes – Effective Data Storytelling

Project forward shows what is predicted to occur in the future. Whereas the rest of the story points are primarily focused on what has happened, this story point forecasts what may occur at some point in the future. For example, you could highlight the forecasted growth of a city's population over the next five years.

Compare and contrast exposes the similarities or differences between two or more items. For example, you may contrast the overall equipment effectiveness rates of two factories—one that has been recently updated and the other that needs upgrading. This story point is probably the most popular type and is frequently featured in most data stories. Facilitating simple comparisons will be a key focus of the next chapter.

Drill down moves from a higher-level or aggregated view of a metric to a more detailed view. Essentially, you break down an overall number by different dimensions of varying levels of granularity. For example, you may start with sales results at a national level and then drill into the regional or individual store-level results.

Zoom out moves in the opposite direction of the drill down story point, expanding from a more granular view to a more aggregated view. For example, you may start with an individual store's sales results and then position its results alongside cohorts in the same region or in terms of national store averages.

Cluster reveals a concentrated grouping or distribution of results within a dataset. A large concentration in one area may indicate an opportunity or problem. For example, you may show how your hospital's costliest segment of patients is comprised of smokers.

Outlier uncovers an anomaly that differs dramatically from other data points. An aberration or deviation from the norm can highlight either an opportunity or problem, depending on the context. For example, you may display how, in terms of repeat purchases, a specific product significantly outperforms all others in a product line.

6 Argue With Data

*No one has ever made a decision because of a **number**. They need a **story**.*
– Daniel Kahneman

6.1 Explore to explain

The purpose of data visualization is to:
Explain: convey information to others (through a single experience).
Explore: facilitate reasoning of data (through many different experiences).
Exhibit: use data as the basis of expression (through infinite experiences).

An analysis is a two-step process with an exploratory and an explanatory phase. To create a powerful data story, you must effectively move from data discovery (finding the insight) to data communication.

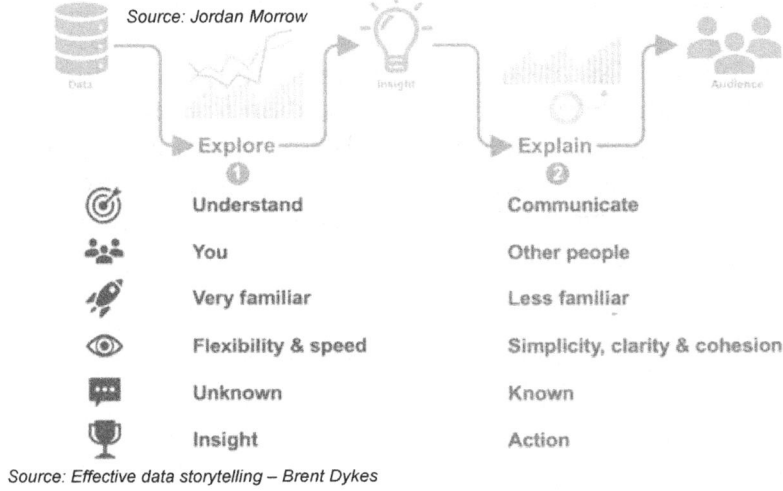

Source: Effective data storytelling – Brent Dykes

There are three pitfalls to avoid: the data cut, the data cameo, and the data decoration. The following sections focus in on each of these pitfalls.

Argue With Data

6.1.1 The data cut
A data cut immediately starts by exploring the data for insights. However, it fails to convey the insight through use of an effective story and explanatory visualizations. It is an example of the "curse of knowledge" cognitive bias.

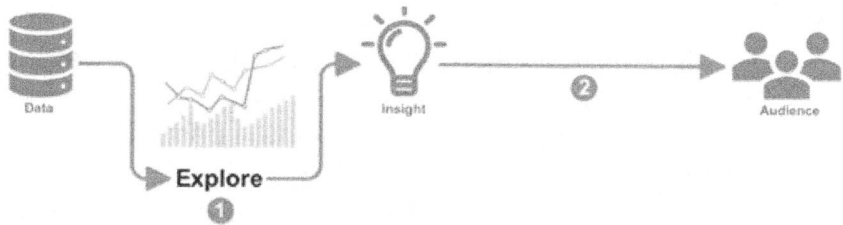

Source: Effective data storytelling – Brent Dykes

This may occur when:
- You feel the data speaks for itself because the evidence is so strong.
- You aren't sure how the audience will receive or interpret the results.
- You haven't spent much time tailoring your charts to your audience.

6.1.2 The data cameo
This occurs when you already know the narrative you want to tell before exploring the data, and therefore select data that supports a particular viewpoint. Conflicting data is ignored, either intentionally (selectivity, omission) or unintentionally (confirmation bias).

Source: Effective data storytelling – Brent Dykes

Business users (as opposed to data experts) are often susceptible to this pitfall. The presentation of the data is often well organized, but the data differs from the source. They often start with a predefined story or, rather an agenda. Data is then added to reinforce the intended story.

This may occur when:
- You already know the narrative you want to tell before examining any data.
- You are selecting data that supports a particular viewpoint.
- You aren't looking to disprove your preferred viewpoint.

6.1.3 The data decoration

This consists of appealing visuals but with a lack of a focused narrative. It happens when you jump too quickly to the layout and presentation, instead of properly executing the explore step. Rather than adding value, this pitfall mainly creates confusion and noise.

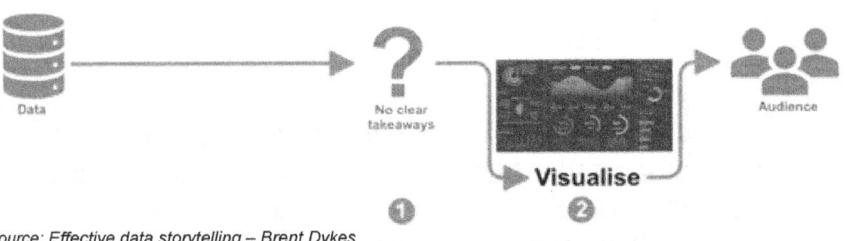

Source: Effective data storytelling – Brent Dykes

This may occur when:
- You don't have a clear focus or emphasis for the visuals you're creating.
- You are more focused on the data visualization tool than the actual data.
- You want to visualize the data so other people with more domain expertise can make better sense of the numbers.

6.2 Effective data visualization

Nobody is born with the capacity to read charts: these are all conventions. The understanding of charts and graphs is learned and developed over time. Charts and graphs are visual representations of data and information, and their interpretation relies on specific conventions and rules established by societies and fields of study. For example, line charts, bar charts, pie charts, and scatter plots are all visual representations used to display data differently. Each type of chart has its own conventions and rules on how data is organized, displayed, and interpreted. These conventions include how the axes are labelled, how data points are plotted, the use of colors and legends, and other design elements.

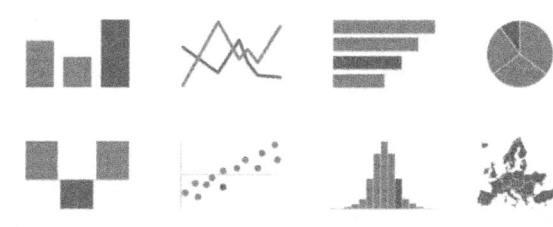
Source: Stephen S. Few, Show me the Numbers, 2004

Be aware of individual differences in visual perception and understanding. Some people have different levels of visual acuity or the ability to process visual information effectively. People may have varying strengths and weaknesses when it comes to visual perception.

For instance, some individuals may find it easier to understand patterns and trends in line charts, while others may struggle with them and prefer bar charts. Similarly, some people may need help distinguishing between different colors used in graphs, making it challenging to interpret color-coded information accurately.

Designing charts that are clear, well-organized, and accessible can help ensure that a broader audience can understand the information being conveyed. This may involve using suitable colors, providing clear labels, using appropriate chart types, and addressing the target audience's needs.

Refer to Chapter 3 for more information on how to choose the correct chart to achieve your goals.

6.3 Storytelling with data

There is no "perfect chart", it all depends on the question you want to answer.

To determine what the question is, always start by asking the five W questions:
- **Why:** To get the real purpose of the question or request.
- **Who:** Who are you doing this for, who is the audience: your colleague, manager, department, company, or external clients? They all have different needs, and they are likely to have different knowledge levels.
- **What:** Our visuals need to focus on signals, not noise. Noise is random, and explaining noise does not make any sense. Also make sure that reading your visuals is as easy as possible for the audience. Avoid indirect measures only. Strengthen you visualization by including direct measures.
- **When:** Time is a great way to show more context, what has happened before, is there a trend, how is the flow, are there ups and/or downs or not.
- **Where:** What type of medium are you presenting the results on? Is it on a smart watch, a mobile, tablet, laptop, a screen, a poster, or even a billboard. And does physical location play a role in answering the questions?

6.3.1 The Storytelling Arc

The four steps of the Data Storytelling Arc illustrate how to tell a data story:

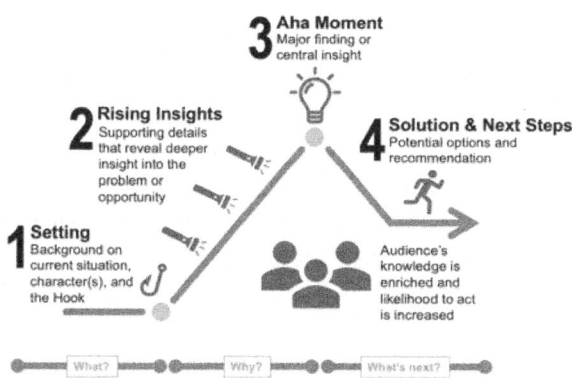

Source: Effective data storytelling – Brent Dykes

1. **Setting:** Background on current situation, characters, and the Hook.
   Provide the audience with "just enough" background information so they can easily grasp the data you will share.
   The Hook: notable observation that acts as a turning point in the story and begins to reveal a problem or opportunity.
2. **Rising insight:** Supporting details that reveal deeper insight into the problem or opportunity.
   The goal is to peel back the layers of the problem or opportunity in a direct and focused manner. You want to include only the information that is necessary to advance the desired narrative because less relevant or tangential findings will weaken your data story.
3. **Aha!-moment (climax):** Major finding or central insight.
   Share the main finding or central insight. Some central insights may be straightforward to explain, but others may need multiple supporting details for the audience to fully understand or accept.
4. **Solution & next steps:** Potential options and recommendation.
   Share how the audience should leverage the new insight. To drive action and change, the "Solution & next

steps" stage is essential to effective data storytelling. Make sure to guide your audience through the different options they have. Proactively suggest a potential solution or discuss next steps, thereby not missing the opportunity to drive change.

6.3.2 Visual storytelling principles

The ability to pivot from exploratory to explanatory in the analysis process is what **separates effective data storytellers from everyone else** who is attempting to share data.

There are seven important principles to visual storytelling, divided into two major sections: the Setup and the Polish.

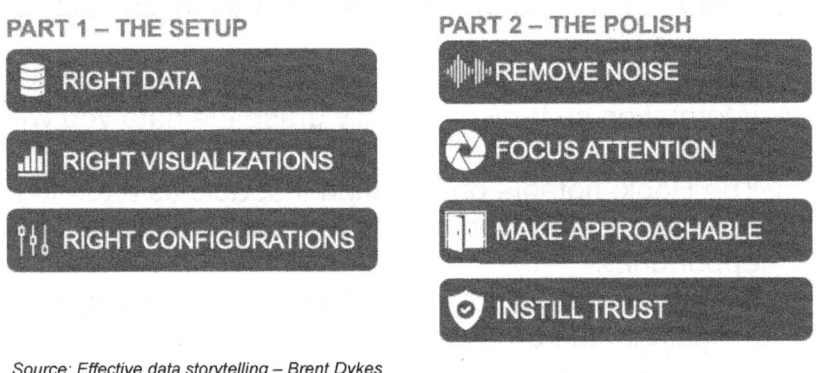

Source: Effective data storytelling – Brent Dykes

6.3.2.1 Right data

Sums or averages do not always communicate your story points effectively. Derived metrics are often better at showing what is really going on. For example, in the figure below we see monthly revenue and customer numbers are increasing for a company. However, only the line chart shows that our revenue per customer is decreasing.

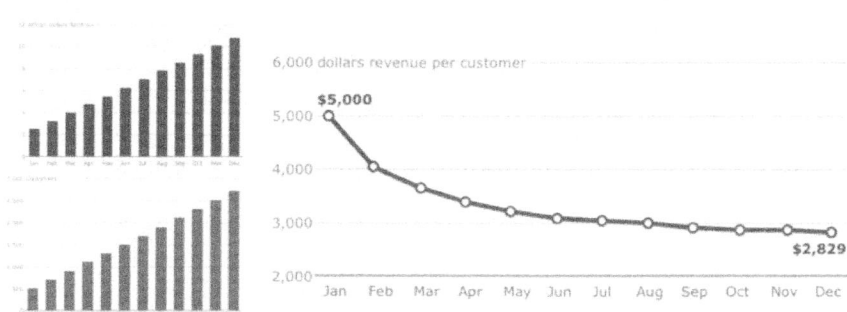

Source: Effective data storytelling – Brent Dykes

Once again, context is key here. Give the reader something to compare the data to. What was the revenue per customer last year? Depending on the context, the message of a single line can vary greatly.

Showing the variance can add emphasis to your key points. Don't let your audience do the math, instead do it for them. Rather than only showing the revenue for two periods, add a chart showing how much they deviate from each other over time. This can give a more vivid portrayal of the expanding gap in revenue, capturing the audience's attention more effectively.

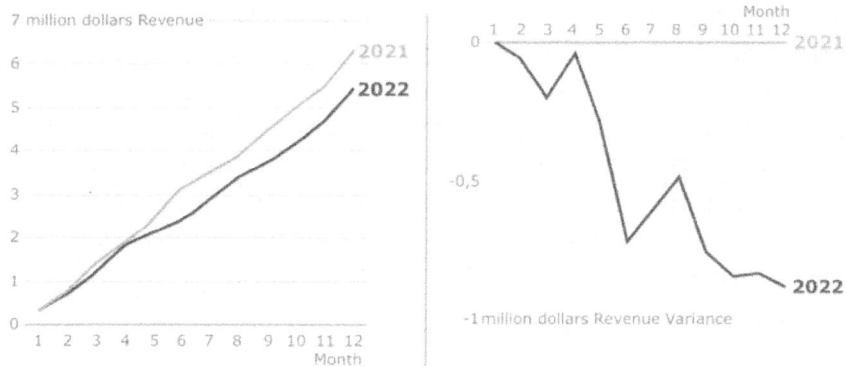

Source: Effective data storytelling – Brent Dykes

6.3.2.2 Right visualizations

Once you've got the correct information, it's time to pick a way to show your ideas using pictures or graphs. But guess what? There are so many kinds of visualizations you can use, and it can be tough to figure out which one is the best. To make it easier, use the previous mentioned CHRTTS model to help you to choose the right visualization for the job.

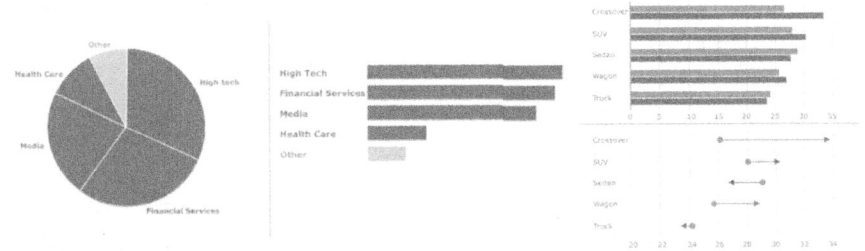

Source: Effective data storytelling – Brent Dykes

If you notice that the people looking at your charts are getting a little bored of seeing lots of bar charts, you can try something different that still shows the data effectively. For example, instead of using another bar chart, you could use something like a dot plot or a lollipop chart. These are possible alternatives to bar charts that can help you show your data in new and interesting ways.

It's important to note that the choice between a lollipop chart and a bar chart depends on the specific dataset, the message you want to convey, and the preferences of your audience. While lollipop charts offer advantages in certain scenarios, bar charts remain a fundamental and widely understood method of displaying data. It's always good practice to consider your audience's familiarity with different chart types and choose the one that best suits your communication goals.

6.3.2.3 Right configurations

Once you've picked the right way to show your data, make sure your chart matches the story you're trying to tell, and ensure your story is as clear as possible.

When you're putting together your data story, you must be sure that each chart you use really supports what you're saying. You must think about how the people looking at it will understand the information and get the main idea you want to share. If there are important things you want people to compare, it must be easy for them to see and understand. You don't want the way you show the data to make it hard for people to get the main points.

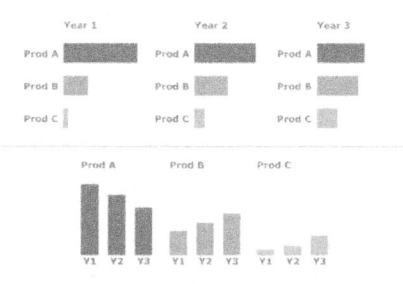

Source: Effective data storytelling – Brent Dykes

When you're checking if your message and visuals work well together, there are three main things you should pay attention to:
- Keep comparisons in proximity.
- Provide a common baseline for comparisons.
- Ensure charts are consistent for comparisons. (same colors and same scale).

6.3.2.4 Remove noise

Don't create noise as you try to visualize your story points. This is sometimes called "chart junk". Some tips to achieve this are:
- Remove surplus data, e.g., hide irrelevant series.
- Aggregate less important data, by creating an "Others" category.

- Separate overlapping data.

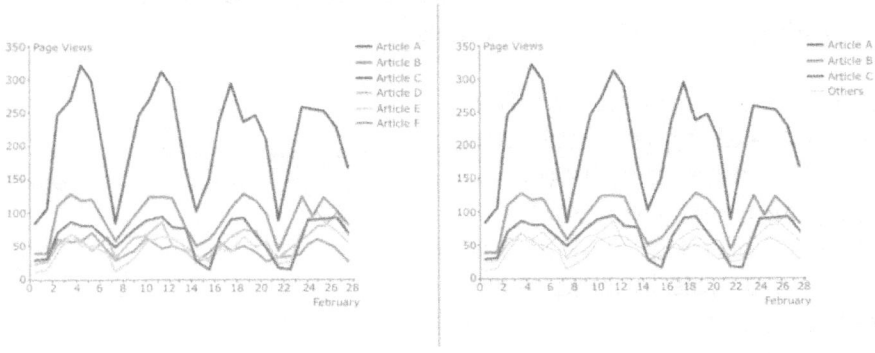

Source: Effective data storytelling – Brent Dykes

6.3.2.5 Focus attention

Even after selecting the right chart type and clearing up the noise, you can still fail to point the audience to the most important information. Place the most important parts of your visualizations in the spotlight so the audience knows what to focus on. You can achieve this by using different colors to make things stand out, or by choosing appropriate data in the foreground and background.

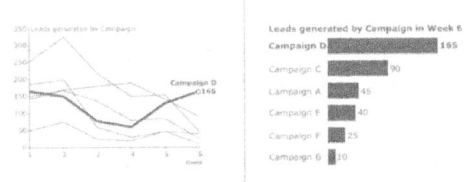

Source: Effective data storytelling – Brent Dykes

Text also plays a big role in guiding people through your presentation. There are two main ways to use words strategically: titles and annotations.

The title of a chart is much like the headline, and it's one of the first things people notice. With the title, you're able to not only describe what's in the chart, but also why it's important. For example, instead of the title saying "Top 10 sales reps by monthly revenue" it could say "7 of the top 10 sales reps are in the Northwest region".

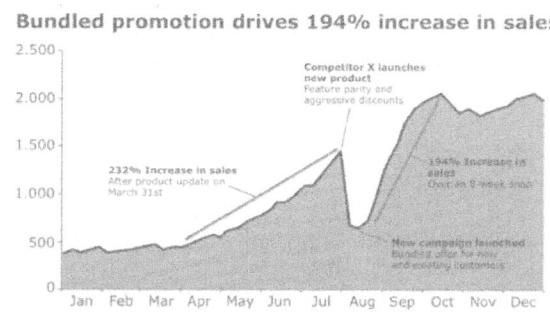

Source: Effective data storytelling – Brent Dykes

Annotations come in two flavours: observational and additive. Observational annotations point out something interesting in the data, such as a maximum value. Additive annotations give additional information that is not visible in the data itself. Take extra care that the text of your annotations is not obscuring part of the data and limit yourself in terms of the number of annotations in a chart.

Finally, consider the role of typography. Your choice in font, font size, boldness and colors can make words or numbers stand out from the rest. This can help direct your audience to the crucial points in your story. Don't use fancy styles for everything, just pick the most important parts.

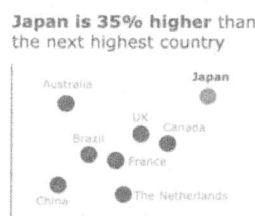 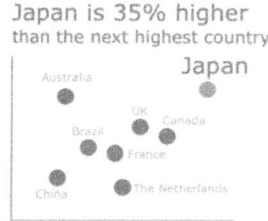 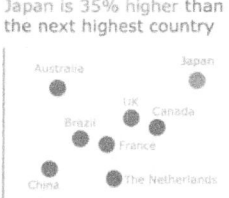

Source: Effective data storytelling – Brent Dykes

6.3.2.6 Approachable and engaging data

When you're telling a story with pictures, good design is like making your story more readable and easier to understand. Design can't make a complicated topic simple, but it can help people follow your ideas and see what you're trying to show them. Pay attention to little things that might not seem

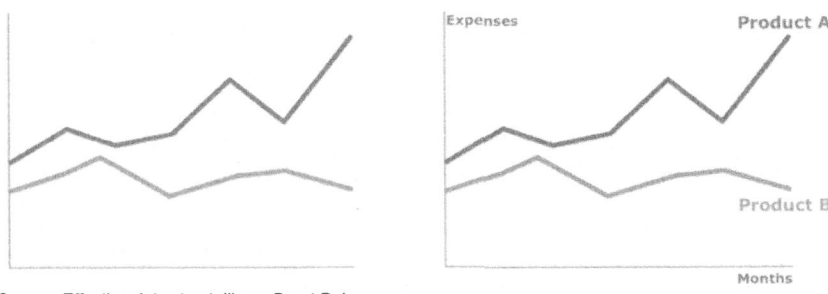

Source: Effective data storytelling – Brent Dykes

important at first. These small things can really make a big difference in how well your visualization works.

Some elements to consider, which can help improve your design:
- **Labeling**
    - Axis labels – use them to guide users through your visualization.
    - Direct labeling – make the lines easier, and more effective to read.
    - Legible text – always place text horizontally.

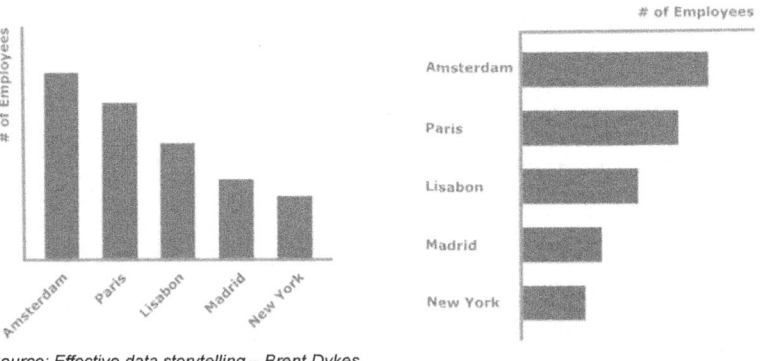

Source: Effective data storytelling – Brent Dykes

- o Simple increments – use natural, logical, and easy to read increments on the axes.
- **Formatting**
    - o Color scheme (monochromatic vs. different colors).
    - o Color blindness.
    - o Order.
    - o Transparency and jitter.

6.3.2.7 Instill trust

Instill trust in your numbers and visualizations. Take care in presenting the truth to your audience by presenting the data in a clear and concise manner.

Be aware of how charts can obscure the truth, so that you can avoid this:
- Truncated axes. For example, in a bar chart, always start the value axis at 0.
- Inconsistent date/time intervals. Don't skip periods on your date, time axes.
- Limited date ranges. Give the complete context of your story.
- Irregular binning. All bins should be the same size.
- Erroneous proportions. Parts-to-a-whole should add up to 100%.
- Missing sources. Display the full dataset.

7 Further Reading

1) Robbins, N.B., & Heiberger, R.M. (2011). Plotting Likert and Other Rating Scales.
2) Kahneman, Daniel (2011), Thinking, Fast and Slow, New York: Farrar, Straus & Giroux.
3) Jones, Ben (2020), Avoiding Data Pitfalls, Hoboken, New Jersey: Wiley & Sons.
4) Few, Stephen (2015), Signal: Understanding What Matters in a World of Noise, Analytics Press.
5) Dykes, Brent (2020), Effective Data Storytelling. How to drive change with data, narrative, and visuals. Hoboken, New Jersey: Wiley & Sons.
6) Wheeler, Donald J. (2000), Understanding Variation: The Key to Managing Chaos, SPC Press.
7) Wheeler, Donald J. (2012), Making Sense of Data, SPC Press.

Made in the USA
Monee, IL
03 May 2026

49438525R00044